Rosa Parks

by Sandy Donovan

Chicago, Illinois

© 2004 Raintree
Published by Raintree, a division of Reed Elsevier, Inc.
Chicago, Illinois
Customer Service: 888-363-4266
Visit our website at www.raintreelibrary.com

For information, address the publisher:
Raintree, 100 N. LaSalle, Suite 1200, Chicago, IL 60602

Printed and bound in the United States at Lake Book Manufacturing, Inc.
07 06 05 04
10 9 8 7 6 5 4 3 2

Library of Congress Cataloging-in-Publication Data:

Donovan, Sandra, 1967-
  Rosa Parks / Sandra Donovan.
    v. cm. -- (African-American biographies)
Includes bibliographical references and index.
Contents: Growing up in Alabama -- Separate lives -- Fighting for equal rights -- Riding the bus -- Don't ride the bus on Monday -- Good times and hard times -- Rosa Parks' legacy.
  ISBN 0-7398-7032-7 (lib. bdg.) -- ISBN 1-4109-0320-6 (pbk.)
  1. Parks, Rosa, 1913---Juvenile literature. 2. African American women--Alabama--Montgomery--Biography--Juvenile literature. 3. African Americans--Alabama--Montgomery--Biography--Juvenile literature. 4. Civil rights workers--Alabama--Montgomery--Biography--Juvenile literature. 5. African Americans--Civil rights--Alabama--Montgomery--History--20th century--Juvenile literature. 6. Segregation in transportation--Alabama--Montgomery--History--20th century--Juvenile literature. 7. Montgomery (Ala.)--Race relations--Juvenile literature. 8. Montgomery (Ala.)--Biography--Juvenile literature. [1. Parks, Rosa, 1913- 2. Civil rights workers. 3. African Americans--Biography. 4. Women--Biography.] I. Title. II. Series: African American biographies (Chicago, Ill.)
  F334.M753P3837 2004
  323'.092--dc21

2003001590

Acknowledgments
The publisher would like to thank the following for permission to reproduce photographs:
p. 4, 58 Reuters NewMedia Inc./Corbis; pp. 6, 8, 18, 21, 22, 26, 36, 38, 52 Library of Congress; pp. 10, 14, 25, 30, 35, 41, 42, 44, 46, 50 Bettmann/Corbis; p. 17 Corbis; p. 28 Seattle Post-Intelligencer Collection/Corbis; Museum of History & Industry/Corbis; p. 32 Highlander Research and Education Center; p. 54 Raymond Gehman/Corbis.

Cover photograph: Bettmann/Corbis

Some words are shown in bold, **like this.** You can find out what they mean by looking in the glossary.

Contents

Rosa Parks is often called the Mother of the Civil Rights Movement. Here, she smiles during a ceremony held to present her with the Congressional Gold Medal, June 15, 1999.

Introduction

Rosa Parks was an ordinary African-American woman in 1955, when she changed history. She was 42 years old and working in a department store in Montgomery, Alabama. At the time, the front section of buses was reserved for white riders only. African-American riders had to ride in the back section. But one day after work, Rosa decided not to give up her seat. She was tired of being treated badly because of the color of her skin. So she refused to stand up, and she was arrested.

By refusing to give up her seat, Rosa Parks began a chain of events that led to better treatment for all African Americans. This woman who was born to poor parents in the Deep South became a symbol to African Americans and oppressed people everywhere that they could make a difference through their actions.

Most of the first black people in North America had been brought from Africa as slaves. Slaves were treated terribly, but even free African Americans were treated unfairly. Even after slavery was

These civil rights protesters hold signs outside a school in 1962.

outlawed, they were still treated poorly. Over the years, many people worked hard to gain African Americans the rights that are supposed to belong to all Americans. These rights include the right to go to school, the right to vote, and the right to be treated fairly under the law.

In the 1950s, the struggle to gain these rights became very strong. These efforts continued for the next few decades and became known as the **Civil Rights Movement.** Many people have made important contributions to this movement, but Rosa Parks is often called the Mother of the Civil Rights Movement.

In her own words: from *Rosa Parks, My Story,* 1992

"Our mistreatment was just not right, and I was tired of it. I kept thinking about my mother and my grandparents, and how strong they were. I knew there was a possibility of being mistreated, but an opportunity was being given to me to do what I had asked of others."

"To this day I believe we are here on the planet Earth to live, grow up, and do what we can to make this world a better place for all people to enjoy freedom."

"What I learned best at Miss White's School was that I was a person with dignity and self-respect, and I should not set my sights lower than anyone else just because I was black."

This photo of Rosa Parks was taken in 1964, when she was 51 years old.

Chapter 1:
Growing Up in Alabama

Rosa Parks was born Rosa Louise McCauley on February 4, 1913, in Tuskegee, Alabama. Tuskegee is a small city and is famous in African-American history. It was the home of Booker T. Washington. In 1881, Washington started the Tuskegee Institute, one of the first institutions of higher learning for African Americans.

Rosa's mother, Leona, was a school teacher in Tuskegee. Her father, James, was a carpenter. The McCauleys owned a small farm in Tuskegee. In those days it was not common for African Americans to own farmland. When Rosa was a year old, her brother Sylvester was born.

It was hard for Leona and James McCauley to earn enough money to support their young family. Rosa's father was often gone for weeks or even months at a time, looking for work. Leona McCauley was mostly alone with her two children. She wanted

Members of the racist organization, the Ku Klux Klan burn a cross in Birmingham, Alabama in 1956.

to get a job teaching, but she had to take care of her children. She decided to move to her parents' farm. Then they could help take care of the children.

Rosa liked living on her grandparents' small farm. It was in the small town of Pine Level, between Tuskegee and Montgomery, Alabama. Montgomery is the capital of Alabama. Rosa's grandparents grew enough food there to feed the family. They grew corn, sweet potatoes and peanuts. Rosa often helped her grandfather on the farm.

Rosa's mother began teaching at the country school in Pine Level. Rosa and Sylvester went to school there. It was a school for African-American children only. The white children went to a different school.

In those days many white people did not want African-American children to go to school at all. They thought they were better than African Americans. Whites **discriminated** against blacks in many ways. To discriminate is to treat someone unfairly because that person is different in some way.

Some white people belonged to a group called the **Ku Klux Klan (KKK)**. The KKK believed that people who were white were better than other people, such as African Americans. But the KKK did more than just think that. They tried to keep African Americans and other minorities from doing things that could help them get ahead, such as going to school or voting. Sometimes they burned down homes, schools, and churches belonging to African Americans. At times, they killed them.

Rosa's mother did not let fear of the KKK stand in her way. She knew how important it is for people to get an education. She made sure that her children learned as much as they could. She told them about how hard people like Booker T. Washington had worked to make schools for African-American children.

Booker T. Washington

Booker T. Washington Junior High School, where Rosa Parks studied, was named after a famous African-American leader and educator. Booker T. Washington was born a slave in Virginia in 1856. When he was nine, the U.S. government freed all the slaves. Booker T. Washington and his family moved to West Virginia, where he was able to attend school.

In 1879, when Washington was 23, he became a teacher. Two years later, he opened his own school for African Americans, called the Tuskegee Normal and Industrial Institute. At the time, there were very few schools where African Americans could get a higher education. The school was in an old church in Tuskegee, Alabama—the town where Rosa Parks was born more than 30 years later. The school taught skills like carpentry and farming. It also trained teachers. The school's name was later changed to Tuskegee Institute. Today it is known as Tuskegee University.

Booker T. Washington gave advice to two U.S. presidents, Theodore Roosevelt and William Howard Taft. In 1902 he wrote a book about his life, *Up from Slavery*. It became a best-seller. He died in 1915, at the age of 59.

Although black and white children were just as smart as one another, the school for black children in Pine Level was not as good as the school for white children. It was only open for six months of the year. The school for white children was open for nine months. And the African-American school did not have as many teachers and books as the white school. It did not have as much money either, so it didn't have as many books and supplies as the school for white children.

Rosa's school was in an old building that was also used as a church. The children had to make sure not to leave their books or papers in the school overnight. They were afraid the **Ku Klux Klan (KKK)** would burn down the building.

School in the big city

When Rosa was eleven, she finished studying at the school in Pine Level. But there were no schools for older children in Pine Level. Montgomery had junior high schools for eleven- through fifteen-year-olds. But most of these were for white children only. There was only one for black children, in a crumbling building in a bad part of town. It never had enough books or teachers for all the students.

Luckily, Rosa's mother had been saving money from her tiny paycheck for many years. She knew that she would have to pay to send her daughter to a private school in Montgomery. So in 1924, Rosa started at Miss White's School for Girls. The students there were all black, although the teachers were white.

Miss White's School for Girls had good teachers and many classrooms with lots of books and supplies. It was very different from the one-room school Rosa had gone to in Pine Level.

An African American drinks from a segregated drinking fountain in the South.

Chapter 2:
Separate Lives

Rosa was excited to be going to a new school in the big city. Montgomery was very different from Pine Level. The houses in Pine Level were mostly one story high and made from wood. Montgomery had huge brick buildings. It had fancy stores with elevators, and public parks and libraries. It had wide, paved streets with streetcars running up and down them.

In the South at that time, white people and black people did not socialize. They were **segregated,** or kept separate by law. African Americans in Pine Level had their own school, their own church, and their own store.

Montgomery was also segregated. Many things were labeled "Whites Only" or "Colored." For example, African Americans could not use the "Whites Only" drinking fountain. Most "Whites Only" fountains had fresh, cool water, but the "Colored" fountains had warm water.

Because Montgomery was so big, Rosa had trouble remembering what she was allowed to do and what she was not allowed to do. She had to remember that she could not buy candy at some stores. She had to remember to look for a seat in the tiny "Colored" section of the streetcar. Often this meant she had to stand, even when there were plenty of seats open in the rest of the streetcar.

Miss White's school for girls

Rosa loved Miss White's School. Miss White was a religious woman who taught her students that they could be anything they wanted to be. She was also very strict. Rosa and the other students were not allowed to dance or wear makeup. Some of the girls did not like this, but Rosa did not mind. She was religious, too. She also wanted to study hard and make something out of her life. She thought about being a teacher like her mother.

But when Rosa finished eighth grade, Miss White's school suddenly closed. For many years, **racists** in Montgomery had tried to close the school. A racist is someone who dislikes large groups of people who are different in some way. In the United States, this usually means they dislike people who are a different color. The racists in Montgomery did not want black children to get an education. For a long time they had tried to scare Miss White into closing the school.

This is a one-room school house in the South in 1926. Before she went to Miss White's School, Rosa attended a school like this one.

Booker T. Washington was a former slave who became an important African-American leader and educator in the United States. This photo was taken between 1890 and 1910.

By 1928, when Rosa was in the eighth grade, Miss White had gotten very old and was not well. She felt she was too old to fight the **racists** any longer. She closed her school that year.

After Miss White's School closed, Rosa went to Booker T. Washington Junior High School in Montgomery. It was not as nice a school as Miss White's, but she studied hard for two years. When she was fifteen, she graduated from Booker T. Washington Junior High.

High school

Rosa was proud to graduate, but Montgomery had no public high schools for African Americans. Rosa had only one choice if she wanted to finish her education. She would have to pay to take high school classes at Alabama State Teacher's College in Montgomery. Rosa's mother wanted her daughter to finish high school and she worked extra and saved money to pay for Rosa's classes.

Rosa hoped to go on to college after high school. But after two years, bad luck made her drop out. First her grandmother became ill and Rosa left school to take care of her. After one month, her grandmother died and Rosa went back to school.

But soon her mother got sick. Rosa had to leave school again to take care of her. Both Rosa and her mother were sad that Rosa had to leave school. But they had no choice. It was hard for poor people to finish school. It was even harder for poor black people.

Raymond Parks

Rosa did not complain about having to leave school to take care of her mother. She thought of it as her job. She found work sewing and cleaning houses. She went to church as often as she could. After a while, her mother began to get better.

Soon Rosa's life changed. When she was eighteen, a man named Raymond Parks asked her out on a date. Raymond and Rosa had met at church. On their second date, Raymond asked her to marry him. They married the following year, just before Rosa turned twenty. It was December 1932.

The Parkses married during a very difficult time in the Untied States. It was called the **Great Depression** and it lasted from 1929 to 1939. During this time, many businesses failed. People across the country were jobless and homeless. Many people went hungry. The Great Depression was hard on everyone, but it was hardest for African Americans.

Luckily, Raymond Parks was a barber in Montgomery. This was a good job, because people always needed haircuts. He kept working even when many other people had lost their jobs. The Parkses found a small apartment in Montgomery and began their life together.

Since her husband had a job, Rosa could afford to go back to school. She started taking classes again. In 1934, when Rosa was 21 years old, she got her high school diploma from Alabama State Teacher's College.

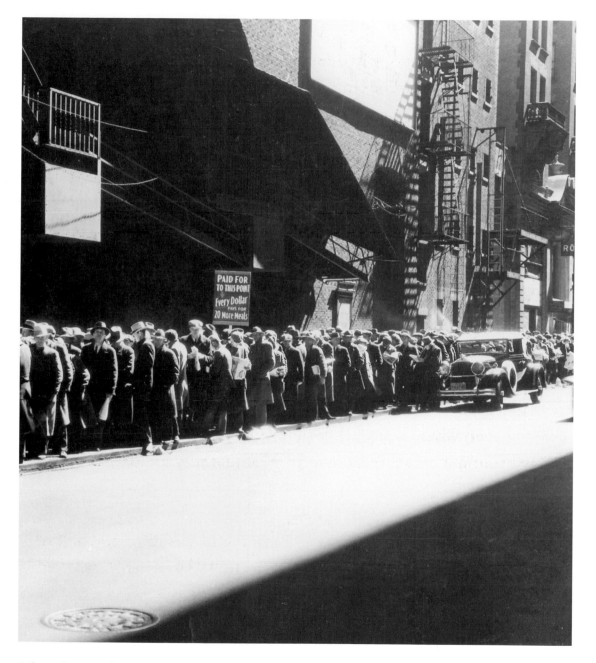

This photo, taken during the Great Depression, shows men waiting in line to buy a five-cent meal.

Many people, including African Americans, found jobs making war materials during World War II. This man tows a new B-25 "Billy Mitchell" bomber at a California plant in 1942.

Chapter 3:
Fighting for Equal Rights

Rosa and Raymond Parks had a happy life. They both worked hard. They went to church often. Rosa's mother came from Pine Level to live with them in Montgomery.

In 1941 the United States entered World War II (1939–1945) against Germany, Italy, and Japan. The Depression ended because the war had created plenty of new jobs in factories. These factories built tanks, airplanes and other war supplies.

Many African-American soldiers fought in World War II. They went to Europe, Asia, and Africa to fight for their country, and some of them died for it. But when they came home to the United States, they were still not treated fairly. Many of them were treated with even more disrespect, especially when they wore their uniforms.

World War II

World War II began in 1939, when Germany invaded Poland. Soon many other countries, including France, England, Russia, and Canada were involved. They called themselves the Allies, and the United States joined them in 1941. They fought against Germany, Japan, and Italy.

The United States needed many soldiers, and the country began drafting young men to fight. When people are drafted, they have to join the armed forces—they are not given a choice.

Thousands of young African Americans went to Europe to fight in World War II. In Europe, they were not **discriminated** against as they were in the southern United States. Most Europeans treated them like any other American soldiers.

In a way, World War II helped begin the fight for **civil rights** in the United States. In 1945 the Allied forces won the war. American soldiers—black and white—returned home. African Americans who had fought for their country were not willing to be treated any differently than white soldiers. They had risked their lives for their country. They had fought for freedom, but when they came home they were not free. In the South, they could not vote. They were expected to sit in the back of the bus. Many of them looked for ways to end **segregation**. And many of them became active in the fight for civil rights.

The first graduating class of African-American pilots in the U.S. Army Air Corps, at the Advanced Flying School in Tuskegee, Alabama, 1942. Though blacks were an important part of the war effort, they still were not treated fairly in the United States.

Getting away with a crime

One day Rosa was riding the bus and saw a young black soldier dancing in the street. He was celebrating because he had just gotten out of the hospital. The bus driver had to brake suddenly to avoid hitting the soldier. This made the driver angry.

A few minutes later, the bus passed the soldier again. He was still dancing in the street. The driver climbed off the bus

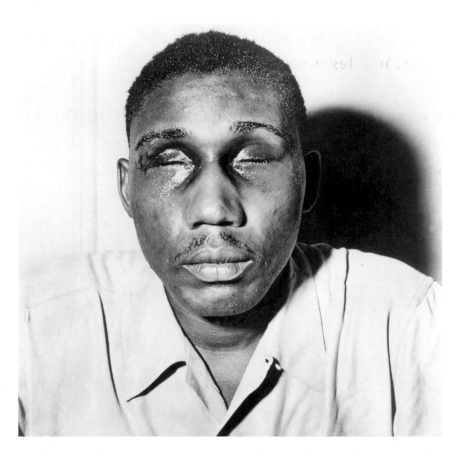

This photo, taken in the 1940s, shows a man who was beaten by racist, white men.

and attacked the soldier. He hit him in the face with his metal ticket puncher. The man's face was bleeding badly. He had to go back to the hospital.

Rosa was angry to see a white man treat a black man so badly, even if the black man had been dancing in the middle of the street. Other people were angry too, and the police arrested the bus driver.

They did not take him to jail, though. Instead, they told him to come to court in a few weeks for a trial.

Rosa went to the courthouse to watch the trial. The bus driver was found guilty of beating the black man. But he did not lose his job or go to jail. Instead, he only had to pay $24. Rosa and other African Americans thought this was unfair. They thought the bus driver was getting away with a crime against an African American because he was white.

Getting involved

Rosa told her husband how angry she was about what had happened. Raymond Parks told her about the **National Association for the Advancement of Colored People (NAACP).** The NAACP worked to gain equal rights for African Americans. Its goal was to end racism across the United States. It had offices all across the country. Most of its offices were in cities in the North, where legal **segregation** did not exist (although **discrimination** against black people was still a problem). The NAACP had a small office in Montgomery.

Raymond Parks had worked with the NAACP for many years. In 1943, when she was 30, Rosa went to her first meeting. She was the only woman at the meeting. Because she knew how to type, she was elected secretary. She began taking notes at her very first meeting. From the NAACP, she learned how to fight segregation.

Spectators line up in Seattle, Washington, to visit the Freedom Train in 1948.

For many years, Rosa had dealt with **discrimination** in Montgomery. She had used "Colored" elevators and water fountains. She could not eat at many restaurants. Now she saw a way to end this kind of treatment. She began to work with the NAACP's youth group. She wanted to help these people fight for their rights.

Freedom Train

In 1948 Rosa got a chance to fight for those rights. She heard that the Freedom Train was coming to Montgomery. This train was traveling through every state in the union with the original U.S. Declaration of Independence and Constitution on board. It was a program of the U.S. government to get Americans to think about their hard-won freedoms at the end of World War II. Everyone would be allowed to visit the train for free, and **segregation** would not be allowed. This was a daring thing to do in the South. But in 1946 the U.S. Supreme Court, the country's highest court, had made segregation illegal on buses and trains that ran from one state to another. President Truman had said publicly that he supported **civil rights,** so blacks and whites were to be allowed on the Freedom Train together.

Still, Rosa knew that Montgomery would try to separate African-American and white visitors. She was determined not to let that happen. She took a group of African-American students to the station to greet the Freedom Train. They stood in line next to some white children. The white teachers were unhappy. But when the train arrived the conductor allowed all the children on together. In Montgomery, this was a big step.

Rosa was proud that the black students and white students had visited the Freedom Train together. But many whites were angry about it. They began making hateful telephone calls to Rosa's house. They threatened to hurt her and her family. It took courage to work for equal rights in Montgomery.

Rosa Parks smiles after a 1956 Supreme Court decision bans segregation on public buses.

Chapter 4:
Riding the Bus

In the 1940s and 1950s, Rosa continued her work with the NAACP. She turned her attention to gaining the right for African Americans to vote. In those days, the law said that everyone could vote. But often when African Americans tried to vote, most of them were turned away. A few did vote, but many of them were threatened by the **Ku Klux Klan (KKK)**. Rosa worked hard to end unfair actions like these, but it was very difficult. Sometimes she felt that African Americans would never earn **equal rights.**

Ever since Rosa had taken the black children to see the Freedom Train, it had been hard for her to find work sewing and cleaning people's houses. Her husband was also losing customers at his barber shop. The Parks family was worried about not having enough money.

In 1955 some of Rosa's friends told her about a place in Tennessee called the Highlander Folk School. This was a place

*Rosa (left) stands at the Highlander Folk School with her mother (middle)
and a friend and civil rights activist, Septima Clark.*

where white and black people got together and talked about how
to end segregation. People from all over the country shared their
experiences of fighting against **discrimination.**

Highlander school

The Highlander school offered two-week summer classes.
Rosa's friends wanted her to go, but she was afraid that whites
in Montgomery would find out that she had gone. She knew
they could hurt her and her family. She was afraid to take the

Highlander Folk School

The Highlander Research and Education Center was founded in 1932 by Myles Horton and Don West. It was called the Highlander Folk School then. Its purpose was to bring together ordinary people who wanted to create a fair world for working people. Horton and West believed that people knew what their problems were. The school's job was to help them figure out what to do about their problems. At first, most of the people who came to the school were union organizers—people who were trying to get better pay for the people working in southern factories and mines.

Even though the Highlander School was located in the segregated South, it welcomed people of all races. In 1953 the school began inviting **civil rights** workers to meet there. After her stay there, Rosa Parks said, "At Highlander, I found out for the first time in my adult life . . . that there was such a thing as people of differing races and backgrounds meeting together . . . and living together in peace and harmony. It was a place I was very reluctant to leave. I gained there strength to persevere in my work for freedom, not just for blacks but all oppressed people."

In 1961 the state of Tennessee closed the school down. The main charge against it was that blacks and whites mixed freely there. That was still against the law in Tennessee. The state took away the school's charter, which had given it the right to stay open. But the school started up again, calling itself the Highlander Research and Education Center. Today, under its new name, it continues its work. It still brings together ordinary people from many different backgrounds. And it still lets them talk about their problems and figure out ways to fix them.

bus from Montgomery, because someone might find out where she was going. So a friend drove her to Atlanta and she took the bus from there.

At Highlander, though, Rosa got her fighting spirit back. She met people from all over the country who believed that blacks and whites were equal in every way. She left Highlander determined to continue fighting **segregation** in Montgomery.

When Rosa got back to Montgomery, she saw **discrimination** with new eyes. She had lived with segregation since she was a child. But now it was even harder to accept just how badly African Americans were treated in the street, in stores, and in restaurants in segregated cities like Montgomery. On public buses, they were treated especially badly.

In Montgomery, black bus riders paid the same fare as white riders. But white riders got to sit in the front section of the bus, or wherever there was an empty seat. Black riders had to pay the driver, then get back off the bus and walk around to the back door. They could sit only in the few rows of seats at the rear of the bus. If those few seats were full, they had to stand, even if there were empty seats up front.

Rosa Parks rides the bus in Montgomery, Alabama.

Keeping her seat

On the evening of Thursday, December 1, 1955, Rosa boarded
a bus. She was going home from after a long day of sewing and
ironing shirts at a department store. She found a seat at the back
of the bus in the "Colored" section. Soon the rest of the bus
filled up.

A police officer takes Rosa's fingerprints after her arrest on December 1, 1955.

Then a white man boarded the bus and could not find an empty seat. The bus driver told Rosa and three other African Americans to stand up. No one moved. After he told them to move again, the other three stood up. But Rosa was angry. She was tired of being treated badly when she paid the same fare as white people. She was angry that everyone went along with this bad treatment. She refused stand up.

The bus driver yelled at her. He told her he was going to have her arrested. Rosa said, "You may do so." The bus driver's face got red. The other passengers were all silent. The driver got off the bus and soon came back with two police officers. One officer asked her why she didn't stand up when the bus driver told her to. Rosa replied with a question of her own. "Why do you all push us around?" she said. "I don't know," the officers said, "but the law is the law and you're under arrest." The police officers arrested her and took her to jail.

At the police station, Rosa was fingerprinted. She asked for a drink of water, but they told her the water fountains at the station were for whites only. Then they took her to a jail cell.

Rosa Parks walks with her attorney on her way to jail in Montgomery in February, 1956.

Chapter 5:
More Trouble

Rosa's family was worried when they found out she was in jail. African Americans were often beaten when they were in jail. Her husband and mother were afraid for her. They called the head of the Montgomery **NAACP.** His name was Edgar Daniel Nixon.

Nixon went to the jail with Raymond Parks and a white attorney named Clifford Durr. They put up $100 **bail.** Bail is money given as a promise that the person will return to court for a trial. After they paid her bail, Rosa was free to go home.

Rosa was supposed to go to court in a few days. She had been charged with the crime of breaking the **segregation** laws. She would probably have to pay $10 as a punishment.

It would have been easy for her to tell the court she was guilty and pay the $10. But what is easy is not always what is right. She talked with Nixon about it. He believed that if she led the way, the **NAACP** could end **segregation.** But she would have to fight in court. She would have to tell the court that the law was not fair.

Rosa knew that many white people would hate her if she stood up for what she believed in. She talked to her husband. He warned her how difficult their lives would become if she said she was not guilty.

Rosa decided not to plead guilty. Instead she was going to challenge the law. This meant a more important court would hear the case. Maybe the case would even go to the **U.S. Supreme Court.** This is the country's highest court. The Supreme Court had the power to rule that segregation laws were not fair. Then Montgomery would have to end segregation.

Stay off the bus

That night, Nixon, her attorney Clifford Durr, Durr's wife Virginia, and Rosa got to work. They all stayed up late talking about what to do. They decided to **boycott** the buses. To boycott means to not buy or use something until it changes in some way. When people boycotted the Montgomery buses, they refused to ride them until they were no longer segregated.

Late that same Thursday night, Nixon called together African-American leaders and ministers from all over Montgomery. He told them about the **boycott** they had planned. Everybody agreed

On February 27, 1956, more than 4,000 African Americans packed into a church in Montgomery to discuss the bus boycott. One of their leaders, the Reverend Ralph D. Abernathy, is shown here speaking to the group.

An empty city bus in Montgomery during the 1956 bus boycott.

to help spread the word. By Friday, more than 50,000 flyers were printed. They all said the same thing: "Don't Ride the Bus on Monday!" African Americans from all over Montgomery helped to post the flyers around the city. They put them in mailboxes, on front doors, and in churches and stores.

News of the **boycott** spread quickly. On Sunday morning, ministers asked everyone in their churches to stay off the buses on Monday. They planned a big gathering at Montgomery's largest black church on Monday evening. This church was called the Holt Street Baptist Church.

On Monday morning, Rosa woke up early. Her trial was only a few hours away. She wanted to be ready. But she also wanted to see how the bus boycott was doing.

Across the street from Rosa's house was a bus stop. On Monday morning, there was usually a crowd waiting there. But today nobody was waiting. When Rosa heard the bus coming, she went to look out the window. She could hardly believe what she saw. The bus was empty. She had expected some people to stay off the buses. But it seemed that every African American in Montgomery had joined the boycott. This bus went through a black neighborhood, and no one was riding.

Support for Rosa

Seeing that empty bus gave Rosa strength to go to court and fight. She knew she was doing the right thing. And she knew that many people supported her.

Rosa arrived at the courthouse with her lawyers, two black men named Charles Langford and Fred Gray. Again, she could hardly believe what she saw. Almost 500 people had turned up to cheer her on. They were mostly black people, but some whites were there as well. Inside the court, Rosa told the judge she was not guilty. The judge found her guilty of breaking the segregation laws and ordered her to pay a $10 fine. Rosa refused to pay and appealed her case to the higher court. That court would decide if the law was unfair.

Rosa's trial got a lot of attention. Here, she is interviewed for the radio before she goes to court to fight her case.

Early that evening, people began gathering for the meeting at Holt Street Baptist Church. Nixon and the other African-American leaders had hoped for a few hundred people. But even before the meeting was scheduled to start, a much larger crowd had gathered. More than 4,000 people turned out that night. They filled the church, the parking lot, and the streets.

A minister introduced Rosa to the crowd. Everybody cheered and clapped for her. Many people gave speeches. The crowd listened and cheered. Then a young minister was introduced. His name was Dr. Martin Luther King, Jr. Most people in the crowd had never heard of him.

King was a powerful speaker. He told the crowd that they must fight hard, but that they must not use violence. He said they had to behave better than the **racists** and the **KKK** members. The KKK and other racists used violence, but African Americans should fight peacefully because they had justice on their side. The crowd cheered.

Rosa Parks and Reverend Thomas Kilgore Jr., in May 1957, after the U.S. Supreme Court ruled that Montgomery's segregation law was illegal.

Chapter 6:
Good Times and Hard Times

After Rosa Parks was arrested, Montgomery's African-American community came together to end **segregation.** The Monday bus **boycott** had been a huge success. The Monday night meeting at Holt Street Baptist Church had been a big success. The city's black leaders decided to keep the boycott going until the city and the bus company agreed to end segregation on the buses.

They formed a group to be in charge of the boycott. The group called itself the **Montgomery Improvement Association** and elected Dr. Martin Luther King Jr. as its president.

Word spread quickly that the boycott would continue. All across the city, black people made plans to stop riding the buses. This was not easy, because very few African Americans owned cars. Almost everybody rode the bus to work. Soon the Montgomery Improvement Association formed carpools. People who owned cars gave other people rides. People who knew how to drive, including some white people, volunteered to help. They made a schedule and started driving African Americans to work all across the city.

Meanwhile the buses in Montgomery were almost empty. African Americans had always been the bus company's biggest customers. Soon the bus company was losing a lot of money. Many stores in downtown Montgomery were also losing thousands of dollars a week. Black customers could not get there to shop.

The bus **boycott** lasted for 381 days—more than a year. **The U.S. Supreme Court** ruled that Montgomery's **segregation** law was illegal. The city and the bus company were ordered to stop discriminating against black bus riders. Only then did the boycott end. Now African Americans could board a bus and sit anywhere they wanted.

Hard times for the Parkses

The bus boycott made life difficult for black people in Montgomery. But it made life especially difficult for the Parks family. Rosa had become famous in Montgomery. Most black people admired her. However, many white people disliked and even hated her.

Soon after the boycott began, Rosa lost her job at the store. At first she did not mind this so much. She spent all her time organizing carpools. But soon her husband lost his job, too. Now the Parkses were worried about having enough money to eat and pay the rent.

Dr. Martin Luther King Jr.

Dr. Martin Luther King Jr. was born in Atlanta, Georgia, on January 15, 1929. His father was a minister and his mother was a schoolteacher.

King started college at Moorhouse College when he was fifteen. When he graduated, he became a minister. He studied the life and work of Mahatma Ghandi. Ghandi was a leader in India who struggled to gain his country's independence from England. He used only peaceful actions to achieve his goals. India became an independent country in 1947. King believed Ghandi's approach could work in the United States.

Martin Luther King Jr. met Coretta Scott while he was studying in Boston. They got married and moved to Montgomery, where King became a minister in 1954. A year later, Rosa Parks was arrested for refusing to give up her seat on a bus in Montgomery. King supported her action and helped organize the bus boycott that followed.

In 1957 King formed the Southern Christian Leadership Conference. This group used peaceful methods to fight for civil rights for African Americans. King's life was often threatened, his house was bombed, and he was arrested. But for more than ten years he worked to end segregation and **discrimination.**

In 1964 King helped organize the March on Washington. More than 250,000 people gathered in Washington, D.C., to demand **civil rights.** King had become the most visible leader of the **Civil Rights Movement.**

In 1968 King walked onto his hotel balcony in Memphis, Tennessee, and was shot. He died instantly.

The bus boycott even spread outside of Alabama. This picture shows a carpool pick-up station in downtown Tallahassee, Florida, in 1956.

Raymond Parks was also afraid for Rosa's life. People were calling their house day and night. Many said hateful things and even threatened to kill the Parkses. It was easy to believe this would happen. In January 1956, Martin Luther King Jr.'s house was bombed. A day later, Edgar Daniel Nixon's house was bombed. In February white students at the University of Alabama rioted in nearby Tuscaloosa. A riot is when a group of angry people run through the streets causing violence and destruction. They were angry because a single black student had been admitted to the school. Raymond Parks was so afraid he became ill.

But even though it had made her life difficult, Rosa did not regret what she had done. By standing up for her rights she had changed history. She was proud of this, and she said she would do it again.

Moving north

In 1957, one year after the bus boycott ended, Rosa and Raymond Parks moved to Detroit, Michigan. They moved in with Rosa's brother Sylvester. Rosa soon found a job as a seamstress. A seamstress is someone who works sewing clothes. Raymond was still too ill to work. For many years, black people from the South had been moving north to large cities. These cities had more jobs and offered a life free of **segregation** laws. By the time the Parks family arrived in Detroit, many African Americans lived there. But even in Detroit, blacks and whites lived separately. Most black people lived near downtown, in older neighborhoods that whites moved out of. Most white people lived in newer houses in little towns around the city. The North was never completely free of **discrimination.**

Still, in Detroit the Parkses no longer received threatening telephone calls. Raymond Parks soon felt better. He began working. Many people knew who Rosa Parks was. Often she was asked to speak at events, both in Detroit and around the country. People who were working for **civil rights** wanted to hear her story.

Thousands of people walk toward the Lincoln Memorial during the civil rights march on August 28, 1963.

In 1963 Rosa attended a very important event. **Civil rights** leaders from across the country asked her to come to Washington, D.C. They planned a march and a huge gathering in front of the Lincoln Memorial. They wanted to push President John F. Kennedy and the Congress to pass the **Civil Rights Act.** This act is really several laws that help to protect the civil rights of some groups, such as African Americans, that have been **discriminated** against.

It turned out to be the largest civil rights meeting that had ever been held in the United States. More than 250,000 people were in the crowd. Rosa Parks and many other famous civil rights leaders gave short speeches. That was the day that Dr. Martin Luther King Jr. gave his most famous speech. It started out, "I have a dream . . ."

This statue, in the Birmingham Civil Rights Institute in Alabama, was made to honor Rosa and her fight for equality.

Chapter 7:
Rosa Parks's Legacy

President Lyndon Johnson signed the **Civil Rights Act** in 1964 and it became law, but **discrimination** did not end overnight. There was still a lot of work left to do. Schools had to be integrated. African Americans had to be able to vote. The biggest gains came during the 1960s. It took the work of many people from all across the United States. Some were famous and many were not, but all of them were important. Dr. Martin Luther King Jr. was one of the best known, but he was far from the only one.

During these years, Rosa Parks continued to work for **civil rights.** In Detroit, she joined the local **NAACP.** At her church, she formed a charity. This group gave food and clothing to people who had lost their jobs. During the day, she still worked as a seamstress.

New job

In 1965 Rosa became office manager for Detroit Congressman John Conyers. Conyers was an African American who had been recently elected to Congress.

Rosa enjoyed her new job. In many ways, it was like the work she had done as secretary of the Montgomery **NAACP.** One of her duties was to answer letters from people in Detroit. Most of the people Congressman Conyers represented were African American. From these letters, Rosa learned what worried African Americans in Detroit the most.

Rosa worked hard at home as well as at her job. She took care of both her husband and her mother, both of whom had cancer. Both were too ill to work. In 1977 Raymond died. Three months later, her brother, Sylvester, died. And then the following year her mother died. It was a very difficult time for Rosa.

Honors

Rosa had no children or other close family, but she was not alone. People across the country loved her. They remembered what she had done in the 1950s in Montgomery. People said that she had helped start the national movement for **civil rights.** In the 1970s and 1980s, she traveled often, giving speeches about civil rights.

In 1979 Rosa won the NAACP's highest honor, the Spingarn Medal. The NAACP has awarded the Spingarn Medal each year since 1915 to a black American for outstanding achievement. Dr. Martin Luther King Jr., Bill Cosby, Colin Powell, and Oprah Winfrey have also won this award.

In 1987 she won the Roger Joseph Prize. This is awarded each year to a person who has made an important contribution to good in the world. This prize came with an award of $10,000. Rosa gave the money to a new organization she had just started, the Rosa and Raymond Parks Institute for Self Development. The institute worked with young people to help them continue their education and realize their potential. Multicultural youth aged eleven to seventeen can learn about the struggle for civil rights and participate in other programs. Rosa hoped it would help young people work hard for causes they believed in. She wanted them to know that they had the power to change lives. The Institute is still going strong today.

National politics

In 1988 Rosa was again involved in making history. That year an African American named Jesse Jackson ran in the Democratic Party's primary. Primaries are the way the two major U.S. political parties select their **candidates** for president. The candidate who wins the primary then runs in the national elections. Jesse Jackson had been active in the Civil Rights Movement.

Rosa looks at her Congressional Gold Medal award, on June 15, 1999, with President Bill Clinton.

The Democratic party chose another candidate, Michael Dukakis, instead of Jackson to run for president. Even though Jackson did not win, millions of voters, both black and white, had supported him. It was the closest an African American had ever come to being elected president. Jackson appeared at a big gathering of the Democratic Party to show his support for Michael Dukakis.

Millions of people around the country watched the event on television. When Jackson walked out on stage, he brought Rosa Parks with him. He introduced her to the crowd and told them that all African Americans "are on her shoulders." He meant that African Americans in the 1980s owed their freedom to Rosa's courageous act almost 35 years earlier.

Living legend

Rosa Parks has received many honors for her work in the **Civil Rights Movement.** Among these are more than 43 honorary degrees from colleges and universities. An honorary degree is given not because someone graduated from the school but to honor important work the person has done. In 1996 President Clinton gave her the Presidential Medal of Freedom. This is the highest honor given outside of the military in the United States.

In 1999 Rosa received the Congressional Gold Medal, another one of the country's highest awards. In 2000 the Troy State University of Montgomery opened the Rosa Parks Library and Museum on the spot where she was arrested more than forty years earlier.

Rosa Parks has accomplished much in her long life. Her courage in refusing to give up her seat on a bus, and bravely fighting for what she knew was right, sparked a movement that ended a great injustice. Since that fateful day, she has never stopped standing up for her beliefs and fighting for **civil rights.**

Glossary

bail money given as a promise that a person will return to court for a trial

boycott refusing to buy, use, or take part in something until it changes. in some way. In Montgomery, Alabama, African Americans boycotted the buses until they were no longer segregated.

candidates people who run for office in an election

civil rights personal freedoms guaranteed to all Americans by the Constitution of the United States

Civil Rights Act several laws that help protect the civil rights of certain groups that had been discriminated against. This act became law in 1964.

Civil Rights Movement name given to the struggle to gain full citizenship rights African Americans. It took place throughout the 1960s.

Democratic Party one of the two major political parties in the United States

discriminate to treat a certain group of people unfairly because of race, religion, or some other difference

discrimination act of treating somcone unfairly because of appearance or other qualities a person is born with

equal rights idea that all citizens–men and women, black and white–should have the same rights and opportunities

Great Depression period of time that lasted from 1929 to 1939, when millions of Americans were jobless and homeless

Ku Klux Klan (KKK) organization that believes white people are better than other people. It has burned houses and churches and has even murdered people to try to keep African Americans and other minorities from gaining equal rights.

Montgomery Improvement Association group formed to run the bus boycott in Montgomery. Members of this group helped arrange other ways for people to get to their jobs during the bus boycott.

National Association for the Advancement of Colored People (NAACP) national group formed in 1910 to fight for civil rights. The NAACP has members of all races.

racist person who believes his or her race, or color, is somehow better than another race

segregate keep separate. In the South, laws kept African Americans and whites from using the same schools, drinking fountains, restaurants, and other things.

segregation system of rules and laws that keep groups of different people, such as races or religions, apart

U.S. Supreme Court highest, or most powerful, court in the country

Timeline

1913: Rosa Parks is born on February 1, in Tuskegee, Alabama.

1924: Begins studying at Miss White's School for Girls in Montgomery.

1926: Rosa attends Booker T. Washington Junior High School in Montgomery.

1928: Rosa takes high school classes at Alabama State Teacher's College in Montgomery.

1930: Rosa leaves school to care for her grandmother.

1932: Rosa marries Raymond Parks.

1934: Rosa receives high school diploma.

1943: Rosa joins the **NAACP.**

1955: Attends **civil rights** classes at Highlander Folk School in Tennessee.

Is arrested on bus in Montgomery for breaking **segregation** laws.

1957: Rosa Moves to Detroit, Michigan.

1963: Rosa attends March on Washington, D. C.

1965: Rosa begins job with Detroit Congressman John Conyers.

1979: Rosa receives the Spingarn Medal from the NAACP.

1987: Begins the Rosa and Raymond Parks Institute for Self-Development

1988: Jesse Jackson honors Rosa by bringing her on stage during the Democratic National Convention.

1996: President Clinton presents Rosa with the Presidential Medal of Freedom.

1999: Rosa receives the Congressional Gold Medal.

Further Information

Further reading

Altman, Susan. *Extraordinary African-Americans*: From Colonial to Contemporary Times. New York: Children's Press, 2001.

Meltzer, Milton. *There Comes a Time: The Struggle for Civil Rights.* New York: Random House, 2001.

Parks, Rosa, with Jim Haskins. *Rosa Parks: My Story.* New York: Penguin Putnam, 1999.

Weber, Michael. *The African-American Civil Rights Movement.* Chicago: Raintree, 2001.

Addresses

The Rosa Parks Library and Museum
Troy State University
251 Montgomery Street
Montgomery, AL 36104
Write for more information on Rosa and the Civil Rights Movement

Rosa and Raymond Parks Institute
for Self-Development
65 Cadillac Square, Suite 2200
Detroit, MI 48226
Write here for information about the organization that Rosa and her husband started in 1987.

The National Women's Hall of Fame
76 Fall Street
P.O. Box 335
Seneca Falls, NY 13148
Write here for information on other women who made history.

Index